Wiccan Holidays: A Celebration of the Wicca Year

By Kristina Benson

Wiccan Holidays: A Celebration of the Wicca Year
ISBN: 978-1-60332-032-0

Copyright© 2008 Equity Press all rights reserved.
No part of this publication may be reproduced, stored in a retrieval system, or transmitted in any form or by any means (electronic, mechanical, photocopying, recording or otherwise) without either the prior written permission of the publisher or a license permitting restricted copying in the United States or abroad.

The scanning, uploading and distribution of this book via the internet or via any other means without the permission of the publisher is illegal and punishable by law. Please purchase only authorized electronic editions, and do not participate in or encourage piracy of copyrighted materials.

The programs in this book have been included for instructional value only. They have been tested with care but are not guaranteed for any particular purpose. The publisher does not offer any warranties or representations does not accept any liabilities with respect to the programs.

Trademarks: All trademarks are the property of their respective owners. Equity Press is not associated with any product or vender mentioned in this book.

Printed in the United States of America.

Table of Contents

INTRODUCTION & BACKGROUND 5
THE SABBATS 9
   SAMHAIN 10
   YULE/ WINTER SOLSTICE 30
   IMBOLC 48
   OSTARA/ SPRING EQUINOX 62
   BELTANE 75
   LITHA/ SUMMER SOLSTICE 84
   LUGHNASSADH 100
   MABON/ AUTUMN EQUINOX 119
The Esbats 134
Index 152

Wiccan Holidays: The Wheel of the Year

INTRODUCTION & BACKGROUND

The major Wiccan holidays, Sabbats, are also referred to as the Wheel of the Year. The holidays of the Wheel of the Year take their names from Pre-Christian Celtic and Pre-Christian Germanic religious festivals. Though the names remain the same, the practices and rituals have changed over the years. Different sects and covens may have slightly different interpretations of the rituals as well. In fact, the complete set of Sabbats were not ever really practiced in the same place in the time until Gardner's book brought them all together and gave them a sort of relationship and continuity.

Today, Wiccans and some Neopagans observe eight festivals which are commonly referred to as "sabbats" or Holy Days. Four of these fall on the solstices and equinoxes and are known as "quarter days"; the other four fall (approximately) midway between these and are commonly known as "cross-quarter days" or "fire festivals". The "quarter days" and the "cross-quarter days" are also referred to as "Minor" and "Major" sabbats, respectively.

The "quarter days" are inspired by pre-Christian Germanic festivals, and the "cross-quarter days" are inspired by pre-Christian Gaelic festivals. However, modern interpretations vary widely.

I have included a list of herbs, plants, incense, decorations, and spells associated with each holiday, a description of what the holiday is honoring, sample rituals, and sample recipes to guide you in your understanding of these holidays.

CAKES AND ALE CEREMONY

Most rituals will have a note about Cakes and Ale. This can be structured as you wish, or not at all. It basically involves enjoying, and making an offering of, seasonal cookies or cakes, and drinks. If celebrating alone, you can simply enjoy the cookies and ale or wine, and meditate on its bounty, and on your blessings. If celebrating in a group, you can all have a feast!

MUSIC

It is appropriate, but not mandatory, to set these rituals to music. I like Loreena McKennit, Mystifier, Three Weird Sisters, Sarah McLachlan, certain Sinead O'Connor tracks, and traditional renaissance or pre-renaissance lute music. If in a group, various members can take turns chanting, beating a drum, or playing an instrument to provide a song for the ritual.

CONSTRUCTING YOUR OWN RITUAL

It is important to note that these rituals are merely a guide. Eventually, you should design your own. If you join a coven, they will no doubt have their own traditions, but you will at least walk into the celebration having a loose idea as to what to expect.

EIGHT MAJOR AND MINOR SABBATS
..and other names by which they may be known

Festival name	Date	The Sun's Position
Samhain (/sawən/), Last Harvest, Blood Harvest, Ancestor Night, Feast of the Dead, Nos Galen Gaeoff	1-2 Nov (alt. 5-10 Nov)	≈ 15°
Yule, Cuidle, Alban Arthan, Midwinter, Winter Rite	19-23 Dec (winter solstice)	0°
Imbolc, Brigit, Brigid's Day, Candlemas, Bride's Day, Brigantia	1-2 Feb (alt. 2-7 Feb)	≈ 15°
Ostara, Earrach, Alban Eilir, Lady Day, Festival of Trees	20-23 Mar (spring equinox)	0°
Beltane, Beltaine, May Day	1 May (alt. 4-10 May)	≈ 15°
Litha, Midsummer, Samradh, Alban Hefin, Aerra Litha, Mother Night	19-23 June (summer solstice)	0°
Lughnasadh (/lunəsə/), Lammas, 1st Harvest, Bread Harvest, Festival of First Fruits	1-2 Aug (alt. 3-10 Aug)	≈ 15°
Mabon, Foghar, Alban Elfed, Harvest Home, 2nd Harvest, Fruit Harvest, Wine Harvest	19-23 Sept (autumn equinox)	0°

THE SABBATS

SAMHAIN

Date: celebrated October 31, or on the exact cross-quarter between Mabon and Yule

Background: The God "dies" on Samhain, and journeys to Summerland to be reborn. The barrier between the spirit world and the "real" world is at its thinnest at this time of year, so it is a perfect time to honor the dead, and engage in deep meditation. Some hold parties for the dead as if the deceased were present; some hold celebrations that honor the dead, but don't necessarily regard them as part of the celebration. Those who engage in chakra work will find this a good time to open channels of communication.

Activities: Some hold memorials for those who have passed, or, as mentioned earlier, memorials with those who have passed. Others use this time for pursuits of divination, such as scrying and tarot. One custom is to light a new orange candle at midnight and let it burn until sunrise for good luck. And, of course, another popular tradition is to carve a pumpkin, put a candle on it, and place it in the window.

Samhain Herbs, Trees, Plants, and Flowers:

Apple
Broom
chrysanthemum
milk thistle
mint
mullein
nutmeg
nuts
oak leaves
pumpkin
sage
thistle
wormwood

Samhain Fragrances and Incense:

Apple
Nutmeg
Sage
Mint

Samhain Colors:

Black
Orange
Red
Brown
Golden yellow

Samhain Decorations:

Jack-o-lantern
Photos of deceased loved ones
Apples
Fall leaves
Autumn flowers
Squashes
Food from harvest
Pumpkins
Skeletons
Marigolds
Pomegranates

Samhain Foods:

Apples
Corn
Nuts
Cider
Mulled cider
Mulled wine
Pumpkin dishes
Pumpkin pie
Cranberry muffins
Herbal teas
Beets
Turnips
Gingerbread
Pomegranates
Meat dishes
Rice cakes
Wheat crackers
Corn muffins
Oat cakes

Samhain Sacred Gemstones:

Jet
Obsidian
Onyx
All black gemstones

Spellwork appropriate for Samhain:

Spells for neutralizing harm
Protection spells

SAMHAIN RITUAL CELEBRATION I

You will need:

An Orange Alter Cloth
Cauldron
2 Black Taper candles
1 Black Votive Candle
1 White Pillar Candle
A plate of seasonal fruits, and bread
Pictures or Mementos of Departed Loved Ones
Mint, nutmeg, pumpkin, or apple incense

Cast your circle, and place one of the black candles on the top left corner of your altar. This will represent the goddess. Place the other on the top right corner to represent the god.

Put the plate of fruit between them. Use your votive candles, then, and take a ritual bath. You may use any sort of purification bath ritual that you wish. When you emerge from your bath and have dried yourself, sit before your altar and enter a meditative state.

Light the incense.

Cast the circle and call Quarters. Invoke the Goddess in her Crone form, and say:

> *"Dark Lady,*
> *crone of the night, Goddess of death and rebirth,*
> *I invoke thee in order to honor and pay tribute to your*
> *black realm. I stand humbly before Thee, asking for Thy*
> *blessing and favor, and that I may commune with my*
> *beloved departed ones as they journey to the*
> *Summerlands."*

Step back from the altar and concentrate on the Goddess candle's flame. Take as long as you wish to concentrate on opening the channels of communication to the Other World. Say:

> *"Dark Father, Consort of the Crone, Lord of the*
> *Underworld, I invoke thee to honor and pay tribute to*
> *your black realm. I stand humbly before thee, and thy*
> *Lady. Keep safe my dearly departed ones as they*
> *journey to the Summerlands"*

Step back from the altar and concentrate on the God candle's flame.

When you are satisfied with your meditation, and that your prayers have been heard, take a piece of the fruit from the plate. Say:

> *"Tonight, into the next world we see*
> *with the living the dead will be*
> *the barriers dividing dead from living will thin*
> *the dead will walk amongst us again*

Cut the apple crosswise with your athame to reveal the symbolic pentagram at the core. Set the apple back on the plate and Say:

> *"Apples and bread for tricks and treats*
> *grown from the earth beneath our feet*
> *to the garden I will go*
> *and sacred apples I will sow."*

Now you will bless the plate of fruits and breads. With your wand, say:

> *To Lord and Lady I give this plate*
> *At my door this feast will wait*
> *In the window a candle will stay*
> *So departed loved ones will find their way*
> *This plate, Lord and Lady, is offered to thee*
> *Bless this candle, this home, this feast.*

Replace the wand on the altar, step back and bow your head. Stay silent for a minute or two as the blessing is given.

Light the black votive candle in the cauldron, and say:

> *Dark Mother, Dark Father*
> *I ask you to bless*
> *The throes of the year as it takes its last breath*
> *The harvest is over, the year is complete*
> *In return for your blessings I offer a feast.*
> *As you wish so mote it be!*

With the flame of the black votive candle light the white pillar candle, saying:

> *In the New Year's wake*
> *Comes new hopes and new dreams.*
> *I hope for blessings to give, and blessings to take*
> *May the Lord and Lady see fit*
> *To offer guidance as my path I make*

Snuff the black votive candle and replace it. Remove the white pillar candle from the cauldron and place it in the center of your altar. Stare in to the flame and think about the goals that you are setting for the upcoming year. When completed the mediation, say:

> *Lord and Lady*
> *To you I beseech*
> *To take my offerings*
> *To hear my speech*
> *Bless us as we light our fires*
> *Bless us as we light the hearth*
> *Bless us as we seek your guidance*
> *Tonight and throughout the coming year.*
> *Blessed Be! Blessed Be!"*

As you say "Blessed Be!" stretch out your arms over your altar to embrace your departed ancestors and loves ones.

When you say "Blessed Be" again, embrace yourself.

Leave one candle burning in your window (so long as you are there to supervise it), and leave the plate of offerings in your garden, or at your doorstep.

Release the circle, and then make merry and celebrate!

SAMHAIN RITUAL II

You will need:

Sage
Spring water
Sea salt
2 white pillar candles
3 tapered candles to represent the goddess, god and ancestor candles
1 piece parchment for each participant
1 pen for each participant
1 black candle for each participant
1 Pomegranate
1 Apple
Cauldron

The person leading the ritual should cast a circle, with the altar in the center. He or she should then light the candle of the person who is in the North corner of the room, or, if you are all outside, the person on the northernmost part of the circle. This person will light the candle of the person next to her, and so on, until everyone's candle is lit.

Then all say:

> *Fire red,*
> *Fire burn*
> *Summer goes*
> *But shall return*
>
> *Fire's flame*
> *Burns and glows*
> *And to us*
> *A vision shows*
>
> *Light the path*
> *To our desires*
> *We chant the spell*
> *O burning fire*
>
> *Night has come*
> *All is dark*
> *Fire bright*
> *Fire spark,*
>
> *Wind blows cold*
> *Red leaves fall,*
> *Rain will come*
> *And Earth takes all*

Fire, water,
air, and earth
The summer dies
To bring rebirth.

Fire warms
The cold within
Hallows eve
Has come again

Now, the leader of the ritual must call the elements.

May we honor the East, Powers of Air,
May we honor the West, Powers of Water,
May we honor the South, Powers of Fire,
May we honor the North, Powers of Earth!

Great Mother and Father
Lady and Lord,
We are asking.
We are listening.
It is Samhain.

Next, call down the goddess. Remember, you are calling to her in her Crone phase. You can call to her as the Dark Lady, Dark Mother, Lady, or Hecate, Calliach, or Morrigan.

You should call her together, and ask for her blessing. At this time, the Goddess candle should be lit.

Next, call in the God. You may refer to him as the Lord or Consort to the Crone, Herne, Horned One, or as Hunter 'neath the Northern Sun. Whatever you call him, tell him as a group that you are honoring his death, and awaiting his rebirth. The leader of the ritual should now light the God candle on the altar.

Then, the leader of the ritual should make a statement of purpose. It can be written beforehand, or improvised. What are your goals for the New Year as a group? Are there deceased loved ones you would like to remember? If so, light the ancestor candle. Invite them, and the Goddess and the God into the circle. It is also important to identify bad habits or practices that the group wishes to shed during the New Year. Time should then be given so that each individual can meditate and reflect on his or her personal goals while gazing into his or her black candle.

At this time, participants can write down goals for the year on their pieces of parchment. This can be awkward, of course, especially if the ritual is to be held outdoors, so it is ok if each participant has written his or her goals beforehand and brought the parchment to the ceremony. The parchments can then be placed in the cauldron, and lit on fire.

The leader should then cut an apple crosswise to expose the five pointed star in its center. The apple should then be passed around so each can take a bite. As it is being passed, the leader of the ritual should say:

> *In living we die*
> *In dying we live*
> *We taste the seeds of death*
> *We taste the seeds of winter*
> *We taste the gift of rebirth*
> *We taste the gift of life.*

After the fruit has been passed around, the circle can be closed, and the deities thanked. The remains of the apple, if any, can be disposed of, but a plate of apples, or seasonal fruits and nuts, should be left as offerings to the Goddess and the God.

If the altar will not be unsupervised for the remainder of the night, the white pillar candle can be lit and left to burn.

SAMHAIN RECIPES

Usually, after the Ritual, a feast or celebration will follow. I have included some recipes that would be appropriate additions to a Samhain potluck or get together.

PUMPKIN GINGER SOUP

1 small pumpkin
1/2 cup cashews
1 tablespoon grated fresh ginger
¼ cup whole milk (optional)
sea salt to taste

Soak the cashews in spring water, covered, overnight. Cut the pumpkin in half lengthwise, remove the seeds and pulp, and bake cut side down at 350 degrees F until very tender. It should take 45 minutes to an hour.

Remove it from the heat, and using oven mitts, scrape the meat of the pumpkin from the peel and puree in a blender, with any juices, in batches if necessary. Blend cashews in blender until smooth and add to the pumpkin puree. Add ginger and salt to taste and heat gently for a few minutes to blend the flavors. If it is too thick, or if you would like a richer flavor, add the whole milk.

VEGAN PUMPKIN PIE

Filling-

1 1/2 packages silken tofu (the kind that comes in a box, not in a tub of water with a plastic cover)

1 15 oz. canned pumpkin

2/3 cup barley malt syrup

1 tsp. vanilla

1 tsp cinnamon

1/2 tsp nutmeg

¼ tsp lemon peel

Pie Crust –

1 1/2 cups sifted unbleached flour

6 tbsp. non-hydrogenated margarine

2 tbsp. cold water

pinch of sea salt

Pre-heat oven to 350 degrees F. Blend tofu in a food processor or blender until smooth. Add remaining ingredients and blend well. For the crust, mix the ingredients, adding more water if necessary, and then mold it along the sides of a pie pan.

After you have blended the tofu stuff, pour the mixture into the 9" unbaked deep dish pie shell. Bake for about one hour. Filling will be soft, but will firm up as it chills. Put in the fridge overnight and serve.

HOT APPLE CIDER

1 1/2 gallons Apple Cider
2 whole cinnamon sticks
5 cloves
1 large orange, sliced thin with peel left on
1/2 lemon, sliced thin with peel left on
1/2 cup sugar

In large pot, combine cider, cinnamon sticks, cloves, orange and lemon slices, and sugar to taste. Serve hot.

Apple Butter

6 pounds tart cooking apples, cored
   & quartered (18 cups)
6 cups apple cider or apple juice
3 cups sugar
2 teaspoons ground cinnamon
1/2 teaspoon ground cloves
1/2 teaspoon ground allspice

In a 8 to 10 quart pot (or Dutch oven), combine apples and cider/juice. Bring to boil; reduce heat. Cover; simmer for 30 minutes, stirring occasionally. Press through food mill/sieve (you should have about 13 cups pulp); return pulp to pot. Stir in sugar, cinnamon, cloves, and allspice. Bring to boiling; reduce heat. Simmer uncovered, about 2 hours or till very thick, stirring often.

Makes about 8 half-pints.

YULE/ WINTER SOLSTICE

Date: Winter Solstice, on or around December 21st

Background: Yule is when the God is born to the Goddess, and it is also the longest night of the year. We use this ritual to honor the God, who has been reborn, and to celebrate mothers, and birth. We perform the ceremony also to call back the sun.

Activities: Many people have a Yule tree, or a Yule log, or both. The log, however, is burned after it is decorated. It is customary to exchange Yule gifts and to make wreaths, and to hang mistletoe over doorways. It is like the Christian celebration of Christmas, in many ways. Remember that some prefer to see the God as two-- the Holly King, and the Oak King. The Holly King is king of the waning or old year, and the mistletoe is representative of the "oak king," the king of the waxing year.

Herbs associated with Yule:

Ash
Bay
Chamomile
Frankincense
Hazel
Holly
Juniper
milk thistle
Mistletoe
Oak
Pine
Rosemary
Sage
Walnuts

Yule Incense:

Bayberry
Pine
Cedar
Rosemary
Juniper

Yule Colors:

Red
Green
White
Silver
Gold

Yule Decorations:

Yule log (oak or pine)
Mistletoe
Wreaths
Strings of dried flowers and cinnamon sticks
Apples
Oranges
Yule tree
Holly
Lights

Yule Foods:

Nuts
Apples
Oranges
Caraway rolls
Mulled wine
Gingerbread men cookies
Roast turkey
Yule Cookies
Pears
Pork
Wassail
Eggnog
White grape juice
Honey cakes

Yule Sacred Gemstones:

Cat's eye
Ruby

Spellwork appropriate for Yule:

Harmonious future
Peace
Tolerance
Respect
Love
Unity

YULE RITUAL I

You Will Need:

Gold cord
Red or Green altar cloth
God and Goddess candles
Chalice or cauldron
Salt or sand
Athame or Bolline
Appropriate incense
Seasonally colored candle
Matches
Goblet of water
Chalice of wine
White candle
Black Candle
Red candle
Bell
Apple, cinnamon, and honey on a plate
Yule Log

Bathe as usual and anoint with oil of an appropriate scent for the season, and wear green and red robes if you wish. Make sure that you keep them out of the way of the candle, however, and have a fire extinguisher near by just in case!

First, prepare your altar. Put the red or green cloth over it, and then position God and Goddess candles. Add the bowl of sand or salt at north. Put the incense burner and incense at east, and a seasonally colored candle at the south⚹ Add goblet and water at west, your wand at east, and the athame at south along with the matches. The chalice should be at the north. Add a bell to west. Put white candle to the left of the cauldron, a red candle behind the cauldron, and a black candle to the right of the cauldron. Place your Yule Log behind the cauldron at the back of the altar, between the God and Goddess candles. If you wish, have materials to make charms for love, fertility, wealth, and abundance. Put an apple and some cinnamon and rosemary on a plate on the right of the altar.

After you have done all of this arranging, take a seat and meditate. Focus silently on the altar.

Say, to yourself or aloud:

> *Today begins the season of Yule.*
> *Today, the Goddess gives birth to Her son.*
> *Today, the Goddess gives birth to the new year.*

> *As the Lord is born again, the darkness will again wane.*
>
> *Today, I honor the Mother of Earth, the Child of Light.*

The words can be adjusted if you see the God as the Oak King and the Holly King, instead of as one god. The Oak King is the king of the waxing year and the Holly King is the king of the waning year. At Yule, the Oak King takes over, as the days grow longer. The Holly King "dies" and sleeps in the Goddess's womb until the middle of the summer. If you wish to envision the God in this manner, change whatever words are appropriate, and add Oak to your altar.

Then, honor the Goddess and acknowledge the Triple Goddess as you continue to meditate.

Light the white candle to the left of the cauldron, and honor the Maiden. Light the red candle behind the cauldron, and honor the Mother aspect. Light the black candle to the right of the cauldron, and honor the Crone. Thank the Goddess, aloud, or silently.

Pull or cut a hair from your head and place it in the cauldron with the unlit yellow or gold candle. Light it to symbolize the birth of the Lord. Now sprinkle rosemary into the cauldron. Drink to the God Child, and light the Yule Log.

Take salt or sand from the bowl and sprinkle it into the cauldron, as well as wax dripped by the red cauldron. Add water from the goblet, and honey from the plate. As you do this, wish for his blessing, purity, and peace. Ask that he accept your offering, and return to this world.

Ring the bell to mark the coming of the Yule season and the passing of Samhain.

Thank the God and Goddess for coming and put out their candles, and close the circle. Bury the contents of the Cauldron.

YULE RITUAL II

You will need:

A Green Altar Cloth
A Cauldron w/Lid or Cover Plate
Holly Wreath
Mistletoe Wreath
12 stones or crystals of your choosing
1 Black Votive Candle,
1 Green Candle
1 White Candle
1 gold candle
Incense
Bowl of Water w/ Pine Sprig in it
Plate of Sand or salt
Athame
Other Personal Items of choice

This ritual is ideally to be performed just after sunset.

To prepare for the ritual, sweep the area in a counter clockwise fashion.

Place the gold God candle at right top of altar. Place the

white Goddess candle at the top left. Place a pentacle in the center of the altar. Place your Cauldron to the right of the altar, with the votive candle inside it. Place the holly wreath in the cauldron as well, but be careful not to interfere with the candle. Cover cauldron with lid or cover plate. Place the taper candle and mistletoe wreath where they will be behind you at the beginning of the ritual. Use your stones to mark the boundaries of your circle.

After your ritual bath, cast a circle. Stand before the altar and say:

> *Light comes from dark. We gather to honor the darkest night of the year, and honor darkness.*

Take the lid/plate off the cauldron and light the black votive candle inside. Step back from the cauldron and meditate on the blessings you wish to receive from the Holly King, the ruler of the dark half of the year.

Call quarters, start by lighting yellow candle in the East:

> *"Powers of Air*
> *dark comes from light*
> *come to our circle*
> *on this Solstice Night."*

Light the pine incense and place on Pentacle/Center Plate.

Light the red candle in the South:

> *"Powers of fire*
> *Dark comes from light*
> *Come to our circle*
> *On this Solstice night"*

Light the blue candle in the West:

> *"Powers of water*
> *Dark comes from light*
> *Come to our circle*
> *On this solstice night"*

Light the brown candle in the North:

> *"Powers of earth*
> *dark comes from light*
> *come to our circle*
> *on this solstice night"*

Meditate on the past year, and the year to come. When ready to begin, say:

Cold is the air
Dark is the night
But the Mother has birthed
The Child of the light
The child divine
Will return with the sun
So mote it be
Two will be one

Remove the Holly wreath from around the black votive candle. With your right hand, brandish it as if to toast to the four elements, going counter clockwise. This symbolizes the death of the Holly king.

Then present the Mistletoe and the green candle to the elements, slide the wreath over the green candle and place the candle in its holder in the cauldron.

Light the green candle with the black votive candle:

> *Behold the rebirth*
> *King of the Light*
> *Awake now, Great Mother*
> *Join us tonight*
> *Goddess of Life*
> *Bringing rebirth*
> *Mother of all*
> *Mother of Earth*

Take the green candle out of the cauldron and light the white Goddess candle on the altar. Replace the green candle in the cauldron. Say:

> *Honor the Oak King*
> *His bringing of light*
> *Honor the Child*
> *Reborn this night!*

Now is the time for meditation and any spellworkings, drink of ale, or taking some cake!

When this has ended, thank the Goddess and snuff Her candle.

Thank and release the elements:

> *Water, fire, air and earth*
> *Spread the news*
> *Of our King's rebirth!*

Snuff each quarter candle and say:

> *Candle burning*
> *Candle bright*
> *I humbly ask*
> *for blessings tonight.*
> *Bless my brethren*
> *My house, my kin*
> *With the love of the Sun King*
> *I carry within.*
> *A candle for you*
> *My King I do light*
> *In honor and joy*
> *Of your rebirth tonight.*

Snuff the green candle. Take the Mistletoe wreath and place it on the other symbols on the Pentacle/Center Plate. Release the circle. Clean up, leaving the gold God pillar candle in center front. If possible, let the candle burn until morning, but not if it will be left unsupervised!

YULE RECIPES

WASSAIL

4 litres apple juice
Juice from one orange
Juice from one lemon
4 cinnamon sticks or 1 t. ground cinnamon
1 inch-square piece of fresh ginger or 1/4 t. ground ginger
1 t. cloves

Heat all and simmer in an enamel pot on low for an hour, and then serve, garnished with cinnamon sticks.

CREPES

5 eggs
1/4 teaspoon salt
1 1/2 Cups flour
2 Tablespoons sugar
2 1/4 cups milk

Optional:

Shaved chocolate
Lemon peel
Powdered sugar
Orange juice
Apples

Beat the eggs well. Add salt, sugar and flour to beaten eggs to make a smooth paste. Add milk and stir well until thin and creamy. Let sit for 5 to 10 minutes to thicken. Stir again and cook as pancakes with a hot buttered pan. Re-apply small amounts of butter as needed. To serve, you can either add a tablespoon of orange juice to the pancake mix and then garnish with an orange peel, OR you can add a squeeze of lemon juice to the mix and serve with powdered sugar, or you can serve with apples.

IMBOLC

Date: The exact midpoint between Yule and Ostara

Background: The Goddess recovers from the birthing of the God at Yule time, and the God is young, and requiring her protection. Imbolc is a time for purification, and a festival of light and fertility. It is a time to honor the Maiden aspect of the triple Goddess, and to make plans for the future year. Many of the traditions are the basis of Ground Hog day.

Activities: Traditional activities include candle-making and candle-magic, spring cleaning (in a physical and spiritual sense), and blessing the seeds that will be planted in spring.

Herbs associated with Imbolc:

Angelica
Basil
Bay
Chamomile
Cinnamon
red clover
dandelion
dill
Heather
Primrose
Rosemary
Saffron

Imbolc incense:

Rosemary
Cinnamon
Wisteria
Myrrh
Basil
Jasmine
Lotus

Imbolc colors:

White
Orange
Red
Yellow
pink

Imbolc decorations:

Lamps
Brooms
Sunflowers
Daisies
candle wreath
horse shoe
seeds

Imbolc foods:

Milk
Onion
Chives
Garlic
spiced wine
Honey
Apple cider
Springwater
herbal teas

Imbolc sacred gemstones:

Amethyst
Garnet
Onyx
Turquoise

Spell work appropriate for Imbolc:

Catalyst spells
Rejuvination spells
purification spells

IMBOLC RITUAL I

You will need:

13 stones of your choosing
13 candles of appropriate color
goddess candle
God candle
candle of appropriate color
candles to mark each of the four quarters
bread
chalice of wine, mead, or juice

To prepare, place a circle of 13 stones on your altar and with in the circle of stones make a circle with your 13 candles. If you wish, you can scatter seasonal flowers or herbs within the circles. Place your Goddess and God candles on the altar on either side of the circle.

Take your ritual bath, and when you emerge, anoint yourself with oil of your choosing. Light the extra candle- the one that is neither the god or goddess candle, or one of the 13 candles-and meditate on it. When you are satisfied, walk with it, and cast your circle. When your circle, use this lit candle to light your Goddess and God candles.

Then, starting in the East, and going clockwise, use the lit candle to light the quarter candles in the four directions.

Then, to invoke the goddess, say:

> *Mother of all life,*
> *I humbly ask your assistance*
> *in my work.*
> *I am here today*
> *in celebration of your gifts.*

Then, invoke the God:

> *Father of the sky,*
> *I humbly ask your assistance*
> *in my work.*
> *I'm here today*
> *in celebration of your gifts.*

Like the 13 candles, and say:

> *I honor the Lord and Lady*
> *so mote it be!*

As the 13 candles flicker, reflect on the coming of the light, and upon the goddess and the God. Like the incense as an offering. Say:

> *Oh lord and lady*
> *join me now in celebration*
> *and heralding of spring time*
> *and your glorious bounties.*
> *Giver of the harvest,*
> *giver of life,*
> *Blessed Lady,*
> *I honor your power and beauty.*

Take the bread, hold it up, and offer it to the goddess and the God. Do the same with your chalice. Eat the bread, drink the wine, and offer thanks. Say:

> *My lord and lady,*
> *seed becomes grain*
> *grain becomes bread.*
> *This spring will bring new harvest and new life.*
> *The spring will bring the heat of the father*
> *to the womb of the great mother.*

Raise the chalice again, and say:

> *Hail to thee,*
> *and to thy blessings.*

Reflect and meditate for as long as you wish before closing the circle.

IMBOLC RITUAL II

You will need:

A goddess candle
God candle
symbols of the season, such as paper snowflakes, or white flowers
orange candle
chalice of milk
besom

This is a very simple ritual that can be performed alone or in a group. Take your ritual bath, and when you emerge, sit before your altar and meditate after casting your circle.

Light the goddess candle, and say:

> *I honor the maid and the mother*
> *who brings all life*

Light the God candle and say:

> *I honor the father and the son*
> *Guardian of life*

And light the orange candle, and say:

> *Here I welcome the longer days*
> *I honor the waning night*
> *I welcome to earth the newborn spring*
> *I rejoice in increasing light.*
> *I celebrate the Goddess, fair and young*
> *I honor the God, the strengthening sun.*
> *I light this flame, and thankful I feel*
> *For life brought by the turning Wheel*
> *I welcome the God as he awakens,*
> *I honor the goddess, mother, and maiden.*

Take the orange candle carefully into each room of your house, and say:

> *I welcome the spring,*
> *I welcome the light!*

Then, close the circle. You may also wish to leave a broom by the door or corn husk dollies on your doorstep.

Imbolc Recipes

VANILLA MILK

Ingredients:

One cup milk per person
1 tsp honey per cup
1/4 tsp vanilla extract

Directions:

Simply mix, and serve, garnished with cinnamon and nutmeg.

INDIVIDUAL GLAZED CUSTARD

Ingredients for custard:

1 quart milk
4 large eggs
1/4 teaspoon salt
3/4 cup sugar
1 teaspoon vanilla
¼ tsp cinnamon

Ingredients for caramel glaze

1 cup sugar

First, cook the sugar in a saucepan over medium heat, until it has completely melted and is a rich brown. Then pour the sugar into the ramekins or bowls that you will be serving the custard in. Rotate the bowl so that the sugar coats all of it evenly; set aside, preferably in the fridge, so it can cool.

To make the custard, scaled the milk in heavy pan - do not boil. Thoroughly beat eggs, adding salt and sugar. Pour egg mixture into hot milk, stirring well. Slowly bring just to a boil until mixture coats a wooden spoon. Remove from heat and beat until cool. Add vanilla and chill well. When it is time to serve the custard, put it into the caramelized coated bowls. Garnish with cinnamon.

OSTARA/ SPRING EQUINOX

Date: Commonly known as Spring or Vernal Equinox

Background: This is the celebration of the equinox, and the first day of spring. The Goddess is in her maiden stage, and fertile and able to be a mother, while the God is reaching toward His prime.

This is a time to celebrate growth, spring, fertility, and nature. It is a time to renew ourselves and really strive towards our spiritual development.

Activities: Ostara is celebrated by doing prosperity rituals, or to simply collect spring flowers. Many of the traditions of Estora were adopted for the celebration of Easter, therefore, egg hunts, and egg decorating is common.

Herbs associated with Ostara:

Spring wildflowers
Honeysuckle
Iris
Jasmine
Lily
Peony
Rose
Sage
Violet
Willow

Incense associated with Ostara:

Jasmine
Rose
Cinnamon
Nutmeg
Aloe
African Violet
Sage
Strawberry
Lotus

Colors associated with Ostara:

Yellow

Green

Ostara decorations:

Colored eggs

Rabbits

Butterflies

Violets

Ostara baskets

Foods associated with Ostara:

Seeds

Cupcakes

candied flowers

hard-boiled eggs

fruit

ham

Candy

Gemstones associated with Ostara:

Amethyst
Aquamarine
Bloodstone

Spell work associated with Ostara:

Growth spells
Communication spells
Fertility

OSTARA RITUAL I

You will need:

One candle for each quarter
one goddess candle
one God candle
Cauldron
one piece of seasonal fruit
consecrated athame

Arrange your altar as you wish, but make sure the God candle is in the Cauldron. This symbolizes the fact that the God is in the care and protection of the Goddess.

Take your ritual bath. When you emerge, walk towards your altar, and cast a circle.

If you are alone, you may read all of the text, to yourself, or out loud. Groups can take turns reading, or group leaders can read all of the text.

Facing east, and turned each direction, to call the elements and their guardians. Say:

> *Spirits of the East*
> *spirits of air*
> *join us in our celebration,*
> *join us in our circle.*
>
> *Spirits of the South*
> *spirits of fire,*
> *join us in our celebration*
> *join us in our circle.*
>
> *Spirits of the West*
> *spirits of water*
> *join us in our celebration*
> *join us in our circle*
>
> *Spirits of the North,*
> *spirits of Earth,*
> *join us in our celebration,*
> *join us in our circle.*

Turn to the altar, and as you like the goddess candle, say:

> *We honor you, great lady,*
> *goddess of Earth, mother of all,*
> *we humbly ask for your blessing.*
> *As night and day once again*
> *greet each other*
> *be with us in our circle*
> *and help us walk in your ways*

Turn to the altar and as you light the God candle say:

> *God of the sun we honor you*
> *God of the growing light. Guardian of all,*
> *we humbly ask for your blessing*
> *as night and day once again*
> *greet each other*
> *be with us in our circle*
> *and help us walk in your ways*

If you are in a group, all should join hands. Together, say:

> *Candles are lit*
> *The circle is cast*
> *Spring is here*
> *And winter has passed.*
> *May the lady and lord*
> *Bless us today*
> *We seek with your guidance*
> *To follow your ways.*

Meditate before the candles and the altar, and ponder the young God, and his need for protection until Beltane.

When you are satisfied, cut the fruit, and hold it to the air to offer it to the goddess and the God. Take one bite in each half. This is symbolic of your acceptance of both the light and the dark; and both the male and female.

Thank the gods and the goddess for their presence, and blessings. Snuff their candles, thank the elements, and close the circle.

Ostara Ritual II

You will need:

Paper and pen
plant pot filled with soil
Plant, bulb, or seed
Green candle
Bell
Spring water

After you take your ritual bath, and cast your circle, place the plant pot on the floor next to the left side of your altar. On your altar, place your paper, pen, and seed.

Ring your bell, and say:

> *The goddess has broken free from the underworld*
> *the maiden shows her beauty with the springtime*
> *the Sun awakens, the God rises,*
> *and welcomes the spring*

Light the Green candle and say:

> *Now is the time to plant*
> *for it is spring.*
> *Now is the time for renewal,*
> *and now is the time for rebirth.*
> *The past and darkness is cast behind us.*

Meditate for as long as you like. Think of what opportunities are ideas you would like to plant. When you have decided what you would like to do and what your goals are in the coming year. Write it down on paper. when you are finished, say.

> *Lord and Lady,*
> *I plant the seed in your names*

Hold your paper over the light Green candle, and hold it in such a way that you can collect the ashes of the paper. Mix ashes into the soil of your plant pot, and pour some of the spring water onto it. Anoint yourself with the spring water as well, meditating on the God and the goddess. Finally, plant your seed.

Ring the bell again, and now it's time for cakes and ale. Close the circle.

OSTARA RECIPES

CARROT BREAD

3/4 cup white sugar

1/4 cup packed brown sugar

3/4 cup margarine or oil

2 cups all-purpose flour

2 teaspoons baking powder

1 teaspoon baking soda

1 teaspoon ground cinnamon

2 eggs

1 pinch salt

1 cup grated carrots

1/2 cup chopped pecans

½ cup raisins

1/2 teaspoon vanilla extract

Preheat oven to 350 degrees F (175 Degrees C).

Grease and flour a 9 x 5 inch loaf pan. In a large bowl, beat together the sugars and oil. Sift flour, baking powder, baking soda, cinnamon, and salt into the bowl while stirring occasionally. Beat the eggs together, and gradually stir into the batter until everything is combined. Mix in carrots, pecans, and vanilla until well combined. Pour batter into prepared pan.

Bake on middle rack for 60 minutes, or until it tests done. Cool in pan for 10 minutes, and then turn out onto wire rack to cool completely.

HAM AND COKE

1 liter coca cola

5 pounds ready-to-eat ham

1/4 cup whole cloves

1/4 cup dark corn syrup

1 tbsp orange juice

2 cups honey

2/3 cup butter

Preheat oven to 325 degrees F (165 degrees C).

Score ham, and soak in the coca cola for at least an hour, but preferable over night. Then, when you take it out, stud it with the cloves. Place ham in foil lined pan. In the top half of a double boiler, heat the corn syrup, juice, honey and butter. Keep glaze warm while baking ham. Brush glaze over ham, and bake for 1 hour and 15 minutes in the preheated oven. Baste ham every 10 to 15 minutes with the honey glaze. During the last 4 to 5 minutes of baking, turn on broiler to caramelize the glaze. Remove from oven, and let sit a few minutes before serving.

BELTANE

Date: Beltane is the Cross-quarter day halfway between Ostara and Litha.

Background: The God is fully grown, and able to take his Maiden goddess to his bed. Their union is celebrated, and she is impregnated. As such, the holiday is primarily about fertility. This is also a time of extreme vitality, and a time to celebrate blessings by giving to those less fortunate.

Activities: Fertility rites are very popular, such as the maypole. Couples who want to conceive might jump over a small cauldron while holding hands, as the cauldron represents the Goddess. It is also a good time to assess the state of the physical body, and enjoy this time to exercise outdoors.

Herbs associated with Beltane:

Flowers
Angelica
Apple
blue Bell
red clover
honeysuckle
primrose
daisy
strawberry

Incense associated with Beltane:

Frankincense
Rose
Passionflower
Vanilla

Colors associated with Beltane:

Green
Rose
Blue
Yellow
White

Decorations associated with Beltane:

Maypole
Leis
Ribbons
Bells
Strawberries

Foods associated with Beltane"

Milk products
Oatmeal
Cherries
Strawberries
Wine
green salads
sherbet
sweet cakes

Gemstones associated with Beltane:

Emerald
Carnelian
Sapphire
Rose Quartz

Spells appropriate for Beltane:

Spells for fertility
Love
Prosperity

Beltane Ritual I

You will need:
cloth of an appropriate color
God candle
goddess candle
a candle for each quarter
May Day crown (made of seasonal flowers)
Cauldron
firewood, if possible

Prepare the circle by decorating it to your taste. Then after your ritual bath, cast the circle, and call the quarters. As you do so, light the Eastern candle first, and proceed clockwise.

Then, invoke the goddess. Light the Goddess candle, and as you do so, say:

> *Dear lady, mother of all,*
> *we call upon you*
> *as you blossom*
> *and as the Lord opens his arms you.*
> *Maiden of May,*
> *we humbly ask*
> *for you to join us in our circle.*

Now, invoke the God. Light the God candle, and as you do so, say:

> *Horned God,*
> *goddess power and the sun*
> *we call upon you*
> *and humbly ask you*
> *to join us in our circle*
> *as we celebrate your reign!*

If possible, light a fire with the prepared firewood. If this is not possible, however, simply placing a candle in a cauldron will suffice. Either way, it should be near the southern quarter of the circle. As you light the fire, the priestess (if you are in a group) should say:

> *In our circle*
> *I light the flames*
> *The God is here*
> *And strong again.*
> *I offer thanks*
> *For to the Maiden of May*
> *And to her consort*
> *Who begins his reign!*

Now, the priest, or acting Lord, will place the crown of flowers on the head of the priestess. He will say:

> *I praise the lady of the spring*
> *I praise the splendor of the may*
> *I offer to you*
> *a crown of your bounty*
> *the beauty of nature*
> *to your maiden majesty!*

All say:

> *Hail to the lady fair*
> *with flower garlands in her hair!*

If you are alone, you can place a crown of flowers on your own head, and give praise to the lady fair.

After doing so, lay the crown on your altar as an offering.

Now, the great rite may be performed as you wish. It may be symbolic, or literal, however you prefer.

Then, bid farewell to the Lord and Lady, and close the circle.

BELTANE RECIPES

EASY CRUSTLESS CHEESECAKE

1 package softened cream cheese
1 basket strawberries or fruit of choice
6 graham crackers
honey to taste

Chop up the fruit into bite-sized pieces. Toss with the cream cheese until the fruit is coated. Then add a couple table spoons of honey. Serve in goblets, with crumbled graham crackers on top.

VEGAN VANILLA SMOOTHIE

1 package mori-nu silken tofu
5 cloves
cinnamon sticks
1 tbsp honey
½ tsp vanilla

Blend everything but the cinnamon sticks in a blender. Even after everything has been combined thoroughly, continue blending it to give it a whipped texture. Then serve and garnish with cinnamon sticks. It should serve generous portions to two; petite portions to 4. Making it with the light silken tofu is excellent too, and is good for those witches watching their waistlines!

LITHA/ SUMMER SOLSTICE

Date: Summer Solstice

Background: The God is a strong young man, and the Goddess is a pregnant maiden. This is the longest day of the year and the shortest night. It is a celebration of fertility, and of strength.

Activities: On Litha, we celebrate the power of the Sun and do as much as possible in the outdoors, and make crafts from wildflowers.

Litha Herbs:

Basil
Chamomile
Daisy
Elder
Fennel
Lavender
Lily
Mistletoe
Mugwort
Oak
Rose
St. John's wort
Yarrow

Litha Colors:

Blue
Green
Yellow
White
Red
Tan

Litha Decorations:

Dried herbs
Sachets
Seashells
Feathers
Summer flowers
Fruits
the sun
any symbols of the sun

Foods associated with Midsummer include:

Summer fruits
ice tea made from summer fruit
ale
mead
Summer vegetables
Oranges
Cookies

Litha Gemstones:

Emerald
Jade

Litha Spellworks:

Love spells
healing spells
prosperity spells

LITHA RITUAL I

In addition to your usual tools you will also need:

a golden yellow altar cloth
dried summer herbs
cauldron
one cup Springwater
red candle
green candle
appropriate incense
altar candle

To prepare sweep the area moving in a counterclockwise fashion. Mark each direction with the candle if you wish.

Decorate the altar with seasonal flowers, and sprinkle summer herbs in the area in which you will be working.

Place the cauldron in the center of your altar to read Campbell to the right of it and the green candle to the left of it. Put the cup of Spring water in front of the green candle, and when this is done take your ritual bath.

When you emerge from your bath, sit before the altar and meditate. If you wish, play some peaceful music to accompany the ritual. Cast your circle. Pick up your wand, and face south.

Say:

> *I honor the mid-of summer*
> *I honor the sun god*
> *in honor of the fertility of the goddess and the God*
>
> *The sun is bathing the earth with its light*
> *the light has kept growing longer*
> *this is the middle of the time of the light*
> *this is Midsummer Day.*
>
> *The sun is high the light is bright the earth is warm*
> *the wheel will turn again to the time of darkness*
> *but for today, the light is bright, the sun is above*
> *I honor the God with my flame.*

Now, light the green candle to the left of your cauldron. This candle represents the goddess. Say:

> *Blessed Lady of nature*
> *Blessed Lady of the moon*
> *Blessed Lady of the meadow*
> *I humbly ask of you your blessing.*

Now like the red candle. This candle represents the God. Say:

> *Blessed father of all things*
> *Blessed father that nurtures life*
> *Blessed father that plants a seed*
> *I humbly ask of you your blessing*

Now light your altar candle in place in the cauldron. Say:

> *May the Lord of the sun with this candle burn*
> *the trouble, the hurt, and pain.*
> *May you leave me purified*
> *with your warmth and light*

Light your incense, and say,

> *Great goddess, great God,*
> *the two that are one*
> *I humbly beg*
> *by thy Powers*
> *though the sky will soon grow dark*
> *and the darkness will soon grow longer*
> *that you banish darkness from my spirit*

Next, anoint yourself with part of the cup of fresh Springwater, and visualize the negatives melting away. Meditate. When done, face altar, and say:

> *Mother Goddess bless this water*
> *father God bless this water*
> *maybe raise of the Midsummer sun*
> *burn away all that is negative*
> *mother Goddess and father God*
> *May your blessings sustain me*
> *on this Midsummer Day*

With the remainder of the Springwater trace a pentagram on your forehead. Then anoint your lips and say:

May my lips speak the truth of the goddess and the God

Anoint your heart and say:

May my heart seek the truth of the goddess and the God

Anoint your hands and say:

May my hands reach for the love of the goddess and the God

Anoint the soles of your feet and say

May my feet walk in the path of the goddess and the God.

Now, and meditate for as long as you wish. You may also engage in any spell workings. Ideal spell workings for Midsummer include prosperity, fertility, and prayer for particle harvest. Finished by having cake and ale, and release the circle.

Midsummer Ritual II

In addition to your normal tools you will need:

Appropriate colored cloth
one candle to represent the God
one candle to represent the goddess
appropriate incense
bowl of sand or salt
blue candle
goblet of water
pentacle
wand
athame
matches
wet napkins made of cloth
Bell
appropriate oil
ale or mead
plate of Summer fruits

To set up for the ritual, cover your altar with the summer colored cloth. Put your bowl of sand of salt to the north of the circle in which you will be working. At the south of the circle, place your blue candle, and at the West place your goblet of water. Put your pentacle at the north of the circle. On your altar, put your god and goddess candles, wand, athame, anointing oil, chalice, matches, wet napkins, plate and summer fruits, bell, and glass of ale.

Now, take your ritual bath. When you emerge, cast your circle. Sit before the altar and invoke the God and the goddess. You may light your seasonal incense if you wish, and, play appropriate music. Say:

> *The longest Day is here*
> *and the shortest night of the year.*
> *The God and Goddess are at their peak*
> *they are lovers,*
> *and her womb is beginning to swell.*
> *We give thanks for harvest*
> *after today, the darkness will grow longer,*
> *The waning year will begin.*

Note: if you wish, you may add something about the Oak and the Holly Kings. Some wish to see the God this way.

Now, open the ritual. You may open the ritual with song, dance, poetry, or chant. You may play recorded music, or perform music. This is designed to attract fairies, spirits, or other elementals. If you feel any presences, offer the plate of Summer fruits. When you are satisfied, anoint yourself with oil, and dedication to the goddess in the God.

Light the green candle and place it the cauldron. Posted the candle in the cauldron with your ale. Drink the happy couples that you know, or to have in general, and offer a summer flower or token to bless the union of the goddess and the God. Put out the green candle.

If you wish you may now perform the great rite. This is symbolic of sexual intercourse and spiritual merging, and is meant to bless and celebrate the union of the Goddess and the God. If you are performing the rite in a group setting, you have many options. You can perform in a purely symbolic act in which an athame is plunged into a cup or cauldron, or, members can invoke the God in the goddess and engage in actual sex together in front of the group. Other members of the group may engage in meditation during this time, or scatter rose petals on the impassioned couple. If you are alone, you may plunge the dagger into the cup, read a poem, or meditate and send good energy to the union of the goddess in the God. There are many ways in which to honor the union of the goddess on the God; what you choose to do is largely a matter of what you, or your group is comfortable with.

After you have performed the great rite, ring the bell to mark the waning year's beginning. Now, it is time for feasting and celebration. Close the circle, and leave the plate of Summer fruits as an offering to the Goddess and God.

Litha Recipes

Grilled Tangerines

1/2 cup plus 2 tablespoons honey
1/4 cup balsamic vinegar
1/2 teaspoon vanilla extract
1 8-ounce container light sour cream, or crème fraiche
6 firm but ripe tangerines, halved.

Whisk 1/2 cup honey, vinegar, and vanilla in small bowl, saving the sour cream and remaining honey for later.

Prepare barbecue. Brush tangerines generously with half of glaze. Grill them, turning occasionally, for about 4 minutes.

When they are done, drizzle with the remaining glaze, and a mound of sour cream/crème fraiche.

Makes 6 servings.

ORANGE BUTTER WITH HONEY

Ingredients:

2 Tablespoons Grated Orange Rind
3 Tablespoons Powdered Sugar
1/2 cup Unsalted Butter
1 Tablespoon honey

Combine the orange rind, powdered sugar, butter and honey in a small bowl. Make sure all of the ingredients are at room temperature. Whip them until the butter is fluffly, and all have been blended.

BERRY FOOL

Ingredients:

4 cups blueberries, blackberries, strawberries, huckleberries, etc
1/4 cup Water
2 cups Sugar
½ cup whipping cream
brown sugar to taste

Cook the berries in water to soften them. When they have become soft and sugar, put them in a blender and mix them so they are all mashed up. Then beat the sugar into them. As they cool, beat the whipped cream until it is stiff. When they cool, mix the berries with the whipped cream and serve in wineglasses, saving enough so each can have a dollop of whipped cream on top, sprinkled with brown sugar.

LUGHNASSADH

Date: The exact cross-quarter between Midsummer and Mabon

Background:

The God begins to die, and the power of the sun is waning, but he is at peace because he will be reborn at Yule. The Goddess is sad because they will be apart, but joyful because she is pregnant.

The focus of this holiday is to give thanks and engage in reflection. It is a good time to think about what we consume, and what is sacrificed so that we may eat, drink, and have our homes. Fruit and grain are generally harvested at this time.

Activities:

Seeds from fruit are ceremoniously given back to the Earth. Meditation and thanksgiving are also appropriate activities

Lughnassadh Herbs, plants, trees, and flowers:

Acacia
Wheat
Rye
Barley
Blackberry
Calendula
Frankincense
Grape
Heather
Mistletoe
Oak
Rose
Sandalwood
Sunflower

Lughnassadh Fragrances:

Sandalwood
Rose
Aloes
Chamomile
Passionflower
Frankincense

Lughnassadh Colors:

Yellow
Orange
Green
Brown
Red

Lughnassadh Decorations:

Corn husk dolls
Basket weaving
Shafts of grain
Sunflowers
Indian corn

Lughnassadh Foods:

Breads

Cornbread

Cider

Blackberry pies and jellies

Rice

Meadowsweet tea

Berries

Nuts

Turnips

Oats

Elderberry wine

Rice cakes

Wheat crackers

Corn muffins

Oat cakes

Beer/mead

Rice milk

Lughnassadh Gemstones:

Aventurine
Citrine
Peridot
Sardonyx

Spellworks appropriate for *Lughnassadh:*

Spells for prosperity
Abundance
Good fortune
Connectedness
Career
Health
Financial gain

LUGHNASSADH RITUAL I

You will need:

Golden Yellow Cloth For Altar
1 Gold Candle
1 Silver Candle
Appropriate incense
Ear of corn or other seasonal fruit/vegetable
Golden Stones or other Sun Symbols
Cornbread or bread
Cauldron
Apple Cider, Ale, or Mead
Any other personal items of choice

Cast a circle, and outline the circle with corn meal, flour, grain, or sand. Set your cloth on the altar, and decorate it with seasonal fruits and vegetables.

Set the Gold God Candle to the top right of center, and surround it with appropriate symbols—sunflowers, gold stones, or depictions of the Sun or the Sun God. Place the Silver Goddess Candle to the top left of center. If you are alone, place a chalice of cider in the center with a piece of corn bread next to it. If you are in a group, you may wish to have a cauldron, and several pieces of bread. (those who are allergic to corn or gluten may make whatever substitutes they wish, of course).

If you are alone, take a shower or bath or purification. If you are in a coven, it is assumed that all members have bathed before coming to the ritual. Whether alone or in a group, after arranging the alter, sit quietly and meditate for a while. Soothing music may be appropriate.

Cast the circle and call Quarters... Pick up your wand with your right hand, face the North with arms stretched out above head, and say:

> *The Wheel of the Year will forever turn*
> *Snow will cool and sun will burn.*
> *This harvest time, the seeds we've sown*
> *With love and blessing, they have grown.*
>
> *Mother Earth and Father Sun,*
> *The summer solstice has begun.*
> *Father Sun, his death draws near*
> *He will return anew next year*

Place your wand upon the altar and with both hands gesture to the Harvest Vegetables, Grains, and Fruits adorning the altar. If in a coven or group, this should be done by the leader of the coven or ritual. Then light the God candle.

> *Truly blessed all are we*
> *For bounties that we do receive*
> *We offer to our Mother Fair*
> *The bounty that with us you share*
> *And offer too for Father Sun,*
> *I honor Thee, the Two are One."*

Pick up the bread, and offer up to the Goddess and the God, saying:

> *Blessings to the Mother Fair*
> *With you our bounty we will share*
>
> *Blessings to the Father Sun*
> *His passing has now just begun.*
>
> *Bless the corn and bless the bread,*
> *May the Earth's children all be fed.*

Now, Light the Goddess candle.

After a moment of silence, name all the things that you are currently grateful for. With each item that you name, break off a piece of the bread and eat it. Sip from the chalice filled with Apple Cider as well. If in a group, each should say a few blessings, eat their bread, and pass the cauldron or chalice to the next person when finished. When all have said their blessings and drank the cider, take a small handful of flour, corn, rice, or grain, and say:

> *"Guardian of the East, I ask your favor*
> *As your wind ripples the wheat and grains,*
> *Carry seeds upon your back*
> *That they may fall amidst the soil*
> *that is our Mother Earth.*

Blow gently across your hand as if imitating the wind taking the seeds air-born and Say:

> *"I give thanks to the Great Mother,*
> *and her fertile lands and to the Great Father,*
> *Her consort and provider of the sun*
> *Of their blessings I partake and share.*
> *Blessed be this Harvest Night, the givers,*
> *the gifted, and the given.*

Blessed Be our Mother,
from whose womb we come and are fed.
Blessed Be our Father, whose seed plants all life.
As the Wheel of the Year turns"

Now is the time for meditation and spellworkings. If no spellworkings are to be done, release the circle.

LUGHNASSADH RITUAL II

You will need:

Ear of corn, still in the husk
Drum
Athame
Chalice
Cider

This ritual is geared to those performing the ritual in a group, but it can easily be performed alone with a few modifications.

First, the leader of the group begins with the opening exhortation:

> "We gather together on this Lughnassadh night to give thanks for the bounty of the harvest and to honor the Crone and Her ancient Consort. We gather to commemorate and mark the passing of time and the Wheel of Life."

All:

> *Blessed be.*

The High Priest will then make the first offering, sitting before the altar with hands uplifted, and say:

> *"Our Lady of Lughnassadh, you give birth to our bounty, you provide us with the gift of all life. Goddess of Grain, of harvest, Goddess of Corn, we rejoice in the fruits of the fields, and bread from your grains I invoke Thee and call upon Thee, Mighty Mother of us all, descend upon the body of this thy servant and priestess."*

Now the High Priestess will sit before the Altar, next to the High Priest, and say:

> *We are blessed, and accept your fruits, your grains, your soil, your rains. Goddess of the Harvest, Goddess of Corn and Bread, we rejoice in your bounty.*
>
> *I invoke Thee and call upon Thee, Mighty Father of us all, to descend upon the body of this thy servant and priest.*

The High Priest then says:

> *I am the ancient Lord, giver of the Sun, giver of Riches, consort to the Crone. I give you my strength, my life, and my power.*

The High Priestess will say:

> *Let us mark the Wheel of Time and the Harvest season.*

She then takes up athame and the corn, and leads the group counter-clockwise about the ritual area. The High Priest will beat a rhythm on the drum and walk with her. This will be done no less than three times. The Priest and others shall beat a rhythm and all shall chant:

> *All that falls will rise again.*

It is appropriate for members of the group to carry fruits, vegetables, grains, nuts, or candles in the procession.

When the High Priestess is satisfied that the chant should end, she says, holding the corn:

> *I accept this offering and this sacrifice*
> *Let it stand for the God,*
> *And I will give his power, life, and fertility to the Earth.*

As she uses the athame to open the husk, the High Priest should fall. The procession will then put all that they carry in the center of the circle, and heap soil or earth on top of it.

The priest will then rise, and hold up the Chalice filled with cider. He will dip his athame into the cider, and say, with the Priestess:

> *Behold the union which brings forth harvest*

The priestess will then face East and say:

> *Great Goddess, Mother of the Harvest, we taste your bounty and humbly ask for your blessing this Sabbat before you take leave of this sacred circle.*
>
> *Our Lady of Lughnassadh, we pray Thee, bestow upon us now Thy Sabbat blessing as Thou takest Thy leave of this sacred space, leaving us with Thy silent, Summer benediction.*

All:

> *Hail, Farewell, and Blessed Be!*

LUGHNASSADH RECIPES

BLACKBERRY OR BLUEBERRY JAM

2 lb blackberries or blueberries
½ lb rhubarb
2 lb preserving sugar
mason jars

Wash, trim and roughly chop the rhubarb, put it into a pan and cook gently until it starts to soften. Stir in the sugar and when it has dissolved add the berries and bring the jam to the boil. Boil it rapidly for up to 20 minutes to setting point. Cool slightly then pour into clean warm jars, cover, label and store.

(Test for setting point: test the jam by placing a spoonful on a plate, letting it cool and then pushing the surface with your finger: if it wrinkles the jam is ready)

BUTTERED NOODLES

4 hard-boiled egg yolks
2 tablespoons orange flower water (optional)
1/2 cup sugar
1/2 cup sweet butter, softened
1 lb. noodles (any kind), cooked
1 teaspoon dried thyme
1 teaspoon dried sweet basil
1 orange, sliced (garnish)

Beat the egg yolks, sugar, butter, thyme, basil, and orange water in a small bowl until smooth. Mix enough of the butter with the hot noodles to coat the noodles with a golden-yellow color. Garnish with orange slices.

Yield: 8 Servings

HONEY CAKES

2 1/2 cups flour
1/2 teaspoon baking soda
2 1/2 teaspoons baking powder
1 heaping teaspoon allspice
3/4 teaspoon ground cinnamon
1/8 teaspoon nutmeg
1 teaspoon ground ginger
4 eggs, beaten
1 1/4 cup granulated sugar
1/2 cup safflower oil
1 cup raw honey

Preheat oven to 350°F. Grease and flour a 9 x 13 baking pan. Combine all ingredients well, pour into pan, and bake for 45 minutes. Serve unfrosted.

HONEY CORN BREAD

1 1/2 cups cornmeal
1/2 cup flour
2 tsp sugar
2 tsp baking powder
1/2 tsp. baking soda
1 tsp. salt
1 1/2 cup buttermilk
1/4 cup vegetable oil
2 eggs
2 tbsp. butter, melted
2 tbsp. honey
Dash of cinnamon

Preheat oven to 425. Combine cornmeal, flour, sugar, baking powder, baking soda, and salt in medium sized bowl. In small bowl, beat the buttermilk, oil, and eggs. Add the buttermilk mixture to the dry ingredients; mix thoroughly. Pour the batter into a greased 8x8x2 inch baking dish. Bake for 25 minutes. While the cornbread bakes, blend the butter, honey, and cinnamon. Baste the top of the bread with the butter mixture during the final 5 minutes of baking. Serve hot or cold.

BAKED TURNIPS

1 pound turnips (about 5 little)
10 ounce cheddar cheese, sliced
2 tablespoons butter
1/2 teaspoon cinnamon
1/4 teaspoon ginger
1/4 teaspoon pepper

Preheat oven to 350F.
Boil turnips about 30 minutes.
Peel and slice thin.
Layer turnips and cheese in a 9" x 5" baking dish.
Sprinkle each layer with spices and dot with butter.
Bake 30 minutes.

MABON/ AUTUMN EQUINOX

Date: Autumn Equinox

Background: The God is about to die, but he is at peace because he will soon be reunited with the Goddess. The Goddess prepares to grow weak as the Earth will freeze over when Winter arrives. This is the Wiccan Thanksgiving, and is used to engage in spiritual preparation of the "season of sleep."

Activities: Winemaking, and the making of preserves, are common in Mabon because they use harvested foods and is symbolic of the fruits of the year. Meditation rituals are very common for Mabon, and it is a time for remembering loved ones who have passed.

Herbs Associated with Mabon:

Apple
Balm of Gilead
Calendula
Cypress cone
Hazel
Milk thistle
Mugwort
Myrrh
Oak
Orris root
Passion flower
Pine cone
Rose
Sage

Incense Associated with Mabon:

Cinnamon
Frankincense
Jasmine
Myrrh
Pine
Sage

Colors Associated with Mabon:

Brown
Dark red
Deep gold
Orange
Yellow
Violet

Decorations Associated with Mabon:

Acorns
Baskets of fallen leaves
Horn of Plenty
Pine cones
Pomegranates

Foods Associated with Mabon:

Apples
Baked apples
Beans
Blackberries
Breads (especially whole wheat or multigrain)
Cider
Corn
Corn muffins
Cornbread
Grapes and grape juice
Nuts
Oat cakes
Rice
Rice cakes
Roots (carrots, potatoes, onions)
Squash
Wheat crackers
Wine

Gemstones Sacred to Mabon:

Carnelian
Lapis lazuli
Sapphire
Yellow agate

Spellwork appropriate for Mabon:

Spells for protection
Health
Prosperity
Security

Mabon Ritual I

You Will Need:

Altar cloth of appropriate color
A Wicker Basket
A Red Apple
appropriate fruits, breads, and vegetables
A Bell
An Autumn Blend Incense
Any other Personal items of choice

To set up your altar, place the wicker basket in its center, filled with the seasonal foods. Place the apple and an athame to its left. Place the tree branch to the right of the basket. Place the rest of your tools and props according to your personal preference. Take a ritual bath or shower, and when you emerge, cast a circle and sit silently before your altar to meditate.

Light the incense.

When you are ready, call the quarters, if you wish, and then say:

> *I honor the Queen of Autumn*
> *And her noble consort*
> *I am here in this sacred space*
> *To reflect on the equinox and the turning of the Wheel*
> *The Wheel has once more turned, and the change of season begins.*
>
> *The Second Harvest has come*
> *And we have eaten of its bounty*
> *And it is time for you to rest*
> *Go now My Mother and sleep,*
> *Go now My Father and dream of re-birth.*
> *You will be warmly greeted upon your return.*

Cut the apple crosswise, and say, as you lift up the two halves:

> *In endings there will be beginnings*
> *And all beginnings will someday end.*

Put down the apple, and say:

> "As the days grow colder, and the nights last longer,
> I have the memories of summer to warm my heart.
>
> *The flame of the sun is fading*
> *But the flame of the hearth is growing*
>
> *The Mother and her Consort will rest*
> *And dream of his rebirth"*

Sit in meditation, and imagine that within the confines of this sacred space you have created, the seasons are turning, and autumn is upon you. Reflect on the memories of the summer, and on the spiritual preparations that you are making for autumn. Say:

> *When I leave this sacred space*
> *The season will have changed.*
> *I will honor the Wheel of time*
> *And endeavor to walk in the path of the*
> *Goddess and her consort.*
> *Lord and Lady, I honor thee*
> *In your work, and in your rest.*

Pick up the Bell with your right hand, and ring it, to toll the passing of the last season, and then ring it with your left to welcome the autumn. Say:

> *"The turn of the Wheel*
> *Has marked the change*
> *In death is life*
> *In life is death*
> *Seasons pass*
> *And pass once more*
> *I honor the Earth*
> *And welcome the fall."*

It is now time for meditation and spellworking.

If there is no spellworking, celebrate with Cakes and Ale, then release the Circle. Clean up. You are done.

Mabon Ritual II

You will need:

Apple
Chalice of wine or juice

This ritual can take place indoors, or outdoors. Some like to practice this ritual in a cemetery, or in a place that reminds them of a loved one, and leave apples in their memory. If it is not practical to practice outside, you may just as easily do so inside, and include objects and memorabilia that remind you of your loved ones that have passed.

When you are ready to begin, cast your circle, and invite your deities.

Say:

> *Blessed be the season of the second harvest*
> *Blessed be the darkness that will conquer the waning year*
> *Blessed be the waning year.*

Take the apple and hold it in front of you at heart level and Say:

> *In life there is death*
> *And in death rebirth*
> *Blessed be the passed*
> *And blessed be the born.*

Cut the apple crosswise and take a bite. Put it aside to bury later.

Now, to honor the God and the ageing Crone:

Say:

> *Blessed Crone, thank you for your bounty.*
> *Blessed God, thank you for your gift of the grape.*

Now toast to anyone you want, alive or passed, with you or far away. Make sure to toast to the Goddess and the God.

When you are finished, say:

> *Blessed be Mabon, season of bounty.*

Now spend some time in your circle meditating or communing with the spirits that may surround you. Then close the circle however you wish.

MABON RECIPES

SWEET MASHED POTATOES

3 pounds sweet potatoes, peeled, and boiled or steamed until completely soft
3/4 cup milk
2 eggs, beaten
2 Tablespoons melted butter
2 Tablespoons sugar
1 1/2 teaspoons cinnamon
1/2 teaspoon nutmeg

Mix milk, eggs, sugar and spices and blend thoroughly with potatoes using an electric mixer. Spread into a greased 9"x13" pan. You may serve it this way, or you may put it back in the oven to turn a golden brown.

APPLE CAKE

2 cups sugar
1 teaspoon salt
1 1/2 cups butter
1 1/2 teaspoons vanilla extract
3 large eggs
3 cups firm apples, diced
3 cups plain flour
1 cup pecans or walnuts, chopped
1 teaspoon baking soda

Beat butter and sugar until creamy. Gradually add the eggs, and beat well. Combine flour, baking soda, and salt, and then add to the butter and eggs. Stir in vanilla, apples, nuts, and mix well. Pour batter into a greased 9 inch tube pan.

Bake at 325 degrees for 1 hour and 20 minutes or until cake is done.

(con't on next page for icing)

APPLE CAKE ICING

1 stick butter
1/4 cup evaporated milk
1 cup light brown sugar
1 teaspoon vanilla

Heat butter and sugar together over low heat. Add milk and let come to a full boil. Remove from heat and add vanilla. Drizzle over the cake. Sprinkle cinnamon over it if you wish.

THE ESBATS

An "esbat" is a ritual observance of the phases of the moon. Most sects of Wicca celebrate the full moon, but others revel in the dark moon, or even the first and last quarters. Traditionally, the Sabbats are times of celebration, while the esbats are regarded as primarily a time for magical workings and spellwork.

There are thirteen canonical full moons each year, although some years will have only twelve. A "blue moon" is sometimes defined as the the second full moon in a calendar month, although some define it as the second full moon while the sun is in one sign of the Zodiac.

In "The Witches' Goddess", Janet and Stewart Farrar state that the Babylonians considered the new moon to be an indicator that the goddess was menstruating, and thought it would therefore be bad luck to work during the new moon. In traditional Jewish culture, this is the first day of the month, called Rosh Chodesh, and is still regarded by some as a holiday for women.

While the Sabbats are more widely and enthusiastically celebrated, the esbats are an important aspect of Wicca, and for good results in spells, it is crucial to be able to figure out what the moon is doing and how it relates to your magical goals.

During the Esbats, the goddess should be honored, and it is appropriate to give her offerings or give to charity in her name. You can work any type of magick at this time, or, if there are no pressing matters to work on, you can merely honor the Goddess, and try to feel a connection with her.

Your altar during an Esbat ritual can be decorated however you like. A chalice full of water or wine, along with a piece of cake is definitely appropriate if you're not sure as to exactly what to do. The cake symbolizes the Earth, water or wine represents water and the moon. The water or wine and the cake should be blessed and part of it should be buried or put in the earth as an offering.

Personalize all aspects of your rituals—they should be completely made up, and from your heart, unless of course you're in a coven and will be honoring the Goddess along with other coven members. In that case, the coven may already have a traditional ritual to follow. If you worship on your own, however, you can say whatever you like and perform whatever action you like.

The influence of the full moon is effective 3 days before to 3 days after the full moon. Your Esbat ritual can take place anytime during this period. If you plan waxing moon magick, perform your Esbat ritual prior to the full moon. If you plan waning moon magick for your ritual, perform after the full moon. If you don't plan to perform magick, and just plan to honor the goddess, you can perform your ritual the day of the full moon.

List of the Moons

January - Storm Moon
February - Chaste Moon
March - Seed Moon
April - Hare Moon
May - Dyad (pair) Moon
June - Mead Moon
July – Wort or Wyrt (green plant) Moon
August - Barley Moon
September - Blood Moon
October - Snow Moon
November - Oak Moon
December - Wolf Moon

January ~ Storm Moon

This is the Moon the marks the last of the most severe storms of winter.

February ~ Chaste Moon

On this esbat, it may be a good idea to purify yourself, possibly abstaining from any earthly temptations during this month, if you wish, in order to greet the spring with a pure heart and soul.

March ~ Seed Moon

Sowing season and beginning of the new year.

April ~ Hare Moon

The rabbit, or hare, is often associated with Estora, and fertility.

May ~ Dyad Moon

The Latin word for "pair" refers to Castor and Pollux.

June ~ Mead Moon

This could refer to the fact that this was the time to collect hay from the meadows.

July ~ Wort or Wyrt Moon

This is a good time to dry and store wort plants.

August ~ Barley Moon

Persephone, Goddess of rebirth, carries barley at this time as a symbol of the harvest, and mentally prepares for the time in which she will descend back into the underworld, and fall and winter will begin.

September ~ Wine Moon

This moon marks the season of the grape harvest.

October ~ Snow Moon

In many parts of the world, October sees the first snowfall of the year.

November ~ Oak Moon
Oak was a sacred tree for the Romans

December ~ Wolf Moon
This nocturnal animal represents the "night"—or darkest part-- of the year.

The Blue Moon ~ Variable
A Blue Moon occurs when the moon with its 28 day cycle appears twice within the same calendar month. Some consider this to be a goal moon, where one might set goals for oneself.

The Black Moon ~ Variable
A Black Moon occurs when there are two dark cycles of the moon in any given calendar month. The second dark moon is considered a very powerful time to perform magicak.

Full Moon dates 2007

Year	Month	Day	Time	Day of week
2007	Jan	3	13:59	Wed
2007	Feb	2	05:47	Fri
2007	Mar	3	23:18	Sat
2007	Apr	2	17:16	Mon
2007	May	2	10:11	Wed
2007	Jun	1	01:05	Fri
2007	Jun	30	13:50	Sat
2007	Jul	30	00:48	Mon
2007	Aug	28	10:35	Tue
2007	Sep	26	19:46	Wed
2007	Oct	26	04:53	Fri
2007	Nov	24	14:31	Sat
2007	Dec	24	01:17	Mon

Full Moon dates 2008

Year	Month	Day	Time	Day of week
2008	Jan	22	13:36	Tue
2008	Feb	21	03:32	Thu
2008	Mar	21	18:41	Fri
2008	Apr	20	10:27	Sun
2008	May	20	02:13	Tue
2008	Jun	18	17:32	Wed
2008	Jul	18	08:00	Fri
2008	Aug	16	21:18	Sat
2008	Sep	15	09:15	Mon
2008	Oct	14	20:04	Tue
2008	Nov	13	06:19	Thu
2008	Dec	12	16:39	Fri

Full Moon dates 2009

Year	Month	Day	Time	Day of week
2009	Jan	11	03:28	Sun
2009	Feb	9	14:51	Mon
2009	Mar	11	02:40	Wed
2009	Apr	9	14:58	Thu
2009	May	9	04:03	Sat
2009	Jun	7	18:13	Sun
2009	Jul	7	09:23	Tue
2009	Aug	6	00:57	Thu
2009	Sep	4	16:05	Fri
2009	Oct	4	06:11	Sun
2009	Nov	2	19:15	Mon
2009	Dec	2	07:33	Wed
2009	Dec	31	19:15	Thu

Full Moon dates 2010

Year	Month	Day	Time	Day of week
2010	Jan	30	06:19	Sat
2010	Feb	28	16:40	Sun
2010	Mar	30	02:28	Tue
2010	Apr	28	12:21	Wed
2010	May	27	23:09	Thu
2010	Jun	26	11:32	Sat
2010	Jul	26	01:38	Mon
2010	Aug	24	17:06	Tue
2010	Sep	23	09:19	Thu
2010	Oct	23	01:38	Sat
2010	Nov	21	17:28	Sun
2010	Dec	21	08:15	Tue

Suggested Full Moon Ritual

One possibility is to take a moon bath. Doing so takes little in the way of resources—all you do is pour some water into a silver or glass container and place container of water outside under the rays of the full moon. The energy from the moon beams are captured in the water. You can preserve the water for a time after the new moon, if you wish. Whenever you want, you can draw a bath, charge the water, and then pour the moon water into your bath.

Suggested Waxing Moon Ritual

One way to celebrate the waxing moon, in the absence of any pressing magickal workings, is to take deck of Tarot cards and separate them into the four suits and the Major Arcana. Then place the Pentacles in the north, Wands in the east, Swords in the south, Cups in the west, and the Major Arcana in the center. Then ask each element and the God and Goddess to reveal to you what to meditate on or focus on between this time and the next moon.

New Moon Ritual

When there is no moon visible, this is a good time to engage in rituals that honor the crone. It may also be a perfect time to meditate and reflect.

Magickal Workings and the Moons

Waxing Moon— this is the best time to perform magickal workings related to:

Love
Wealth
Health
Prosperity
Friends
Protection
Good Fortune

Waning Moon-- this is the best time to perform magickal workings related to:

Loneliness
Shyness
Sickness
Enemies
Bad influences
Danger

Esbat Recipes

Crescent Cakes

1 cup finely ground almonds
1 1/4 cups flour
1/2 cup confectioner's sugar
1 tsp vanilla extract
2 drops almond extract
1/2 cup softened butter
1 egg yolk
cinnamon

Combine almonds, flour, sugar, and extract until thoroughly mixed. With hands, work in butter and egg yolk until well-blended. Chill dough. Preheat oven to 325°F. Take pieces of dough (about walnut-size) and shape them into crescents. Place on a greased sheet and baked for 20 minutes. Then sprinkle with cinnamon and powdered sugar.

Welsh Honey Cakes

1/2 cup (4 ounces) honey
1 teaspoon cinnamon
1/2 cup brown sugar
1 egg
2 cups flour
1/2 teaspoon baking soda
1/2 cup butter or margarine
sugar
a little milk

Sieve together the flour, cinnamon, and baking soda. Cream the butter and sugar in another bowl. Separate the egg and add the yolk to the butter/sugar mix (reserving the white). Add the honey gradually and mix thoroughly, then mix in the flour mixture with a little bit of milk so that the batter is stirrable but thick. Whisk the egg white into a stiff froth and fold it into the batter. Half fill muffin tins with the mix. Sprinkle a little sugar on the tops. Bake at 425° F for 12-15 minutes, longer if needed to be cooked through.

Yield: 12 cakes
Source: Croeso Cymreig, A Welsh Welcome

Full Moon Cauliflower

1/4 cup butter
2 tablespoons flour
1 cup milk
3 eggs
1 clove garlic, minced
1/4 cup bread crumbs
1 cup grated Parmesan cheese
1 cup grated white cheese
1 head cauliflower, cut into florets and cooked

Preheat oven to 400°F. Melt the butter in a small saucepan over low heat. Mix in the flour to form a paste. Slowly stir in the milk until smooth. Beat in the eggs. Stir in the garlic, bread crumbs, Parmesan cheese, white cheese, and cauliflower. Pour into greased baking dish. Bake for 30 minutes. Garnish with additional white cheese.

Yield: 4 servings
Source: Telesco, A Kitchen Witch's Cookbook

Index

AUTUMN EQUINOX 3, 119
Beltane 8, 69, 75, 76, 77, 78, 79
Imbolc 8, 48, 49, 50, 51, 52, 59
Litha 8, 75, 84, 85, 86, 87, 97
Lughnassadh 101, 102, 103, 104, 110, 111, 113
Mabon 8, 10, 100, 119, 120, 121, 122, 123, 124, 128, 129
Midsummer 8, 86, 89, 91, 92, 93, 100
Ostara 8, 48, 62, 63, 64, 65, 70, 75
Samhain 8, 10, 11, 12, 13, 14, 23, 26, 39
SPRING EQUINOX 3, 62
SUMMER SOLSTICE 3, 84
Thanksgiving 119
WINTER SOLSTICE 3, 31
YULE 3, 31, 36, 40, 46